CROQUET.

BY

CAPTAIN MAYNE REID.

LONDON:

CHARLES JAMES SKEET, 10, KING WILLIAM STREET,

CHARING CROSS.

1863.

LONDON:
COX AND WYMAN, PRINTERS, GREAT QUEEN STREET,
LINCOLN'S INN FIELDS.

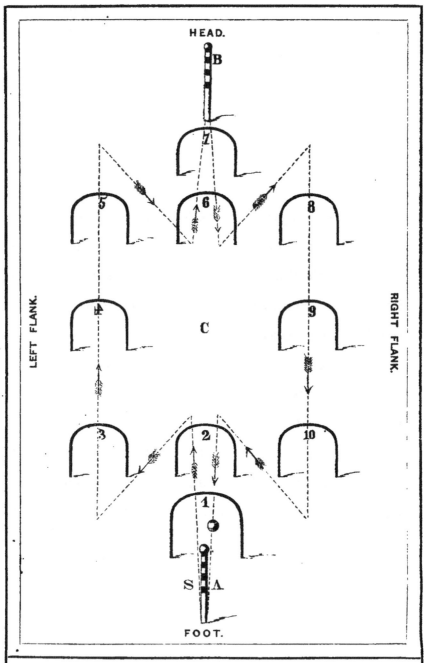

HEAD.

B

LEFT FLANK.

RIGHT FLANK.

5 6 8

4 C 9

3 2 10

1

S A

FOOT.

A. The Starting Stake.   B The Turning Stake.   C The Centre.   S The Spot.

1, 2, Lower Central Bridges.   3, 4, 5, Left Flank Bridges.
6, 7, Upper Central Bridges.   8, 9, 10, Right Flank Bridges.

The Dotted Lines and Arrows indicate the course of a Ball in making the Grand Round of the Game.

PREFACE.

—◦◇◦—

It is not more than truth to say, that CROQUET is the most attractive pastime of the age; while, in point of *intellectuality*, it will dispute the palm with billiards or whist—perhaps, even with that selfish duality, chess.

No doubt, the zealous devotee, of any of the above-mentioned games, will question the honesty of this assertion; but he must be indeed strongly wedded to the habits of his own *spécialité*, if, after being brought within reach of its influence, he do not surrender to the seductions of the charmer—Croquet.

In sober earnest, there are many points in which this game stands pre-eminent; and were it our purpose to prove its pre-eminence, the task would be easy of accomplishment. The quick growth of its popularity—still constantly and rapidly increasing—is proof of the superior attractiveness of the game; and may justify the prediction: that croquet is destined, at no distant day, to become, not only the national sport of England, but the *pastime of the age*.

Unlike the games already mentioned, it is a sport of the open air, and therefore highly conducive to health; while it has the advantage of most other out-door amusements—in affording an easy exercise to the body, without requiring the violent muscular exertion which renders many of these objectionable.

Neither is the mind neglected in the play of this accommodating pastime. Its rules are so varied, yet so rational, that the intellect is constantly kept on the alert,—never summoned to a painful stretch, and never allowed to subside into an equally painful inaction.

It is adapted to people of all ages, and every condition. The child just entering upon the walk of life, and the old man tottering towards its end, may play a "round" of croquet, with equally childish delight.

Nor is its skill exclusive to either sex. The pretty *mignon* foot, piquantly encased in kid, may exhibit as much power in the play, as the thick-soled *chaussure* of calfskin. Ah! we might name more than one fair owner of such provoking feet who could send you—*per croquet*—to "Hong Kong," or "up the country" with as much velocity, as if you had been projected *ex pede Hercul*-is.

Though hitherto restricted to the lawn of the lordly mansion, and confined within the palings of the park, "croquet" will ere long escape from aristocratic keeping; and become equally the property of the paddock, and the village green.

Let us hope that no class-jealousy will arise to prevent its spread, or lessen its attractiveness, to those who were the first to introduce and enjoy it. Croquet is an innocent amusement—a game of true civilizing influences. While deserving every epithet of praise—worthy of being designated the "king of games," the "queen of sports," or the "prince of pastimes"—let us hope that it may also become a *pastime of the people*.

Rejoicing in this hope, I neither feel reluctance, nor make apology, for putting myself forward as its advocate and expounder.

MAYNE REID.

THE RANCHE,
GERRARD'S CROSS, BUCKS.

CROQUET.

———◦○◦○◦○◦———

CHAPTER I.

The Slang.

CROQUET.—The title of the game.

CROQUETERIE.—The implements, viz.:—*Balls, bridges, mallets,* and *stakes.*

ROQUET.—A ball makes "roquet" when, proceeding from a blow of the mallet, it comes in contact with another ball.

RE-ROQUET.—To roquet the same ball twice, without any intervening action of the play.

THE CROQUET.—A ball, having made roquet on another, is taken up, and placed in contact with the ball on which it has roque'd. The player sets foot upon the former; presses firmly, so as to hold it in place; and, with a blow of the mallet, drives the roque'd ball in whatever direction may be desired.[1]

---

[1] The operation of "croque'ing," or *cracking* the balls, being one of the most important in the play, has given its title to the game. It is usual for the player, while holding the ball under foot, to rest the heel upon the ground. This is a matter of choice; as is also the foot to be used. Either will answer the requirements of the game,.

ROQUET-CROQUET, OR CROQUET SANS PIED.—A ball having made roquet, is taken up; placed contiguous to the roque'd ball; and, without being held under the foot, is struck by the mallet, and driven—as also the roque'd ball—in the direction desired.[2]

RICOCHET.—A ball making roquet on two or more balls, by the same blow of the mallet.[3]

CONCUSSION.—The displacement of a ball by another—driven against it by roquet, croquet, ricochet, or roquet-croquet; and not hit directly, either by the mallet or the playing ball.

A BLOW.—The stroke of the mallet.

A PUSH.—When the player presses the ball forward with the mallet, instead of giving it a *blow*.[4]

A POINT.—Making a success, viz.:—a *point* in the game.

A DOUBLE-POINT.—Two points made by the same blow of the mallet.

A FLUKE.—When a point is made, not due to the skill of the player.

A FLINCH.—When the ball in the act of "croquet," at the blow of the mallet, glides from under the foot of the player.

A TOUR OF PLAY. — Is the turn given to each player. It *continues* so long as a point is made, and *terminates* with a failure.

---

[2] Upon some croquet-grounds this operation is called "taking two turns"—the playing ball, after making the collision, having the right to continue its play. This appellation, however, is as little rational as it is euphonious: since the croquet itself possesses the same privilege.

Roquet-croquet is simply a *croquet*, without the *interposition* of the foot. As will be found in the "Rules," it is only allowable under certain circumstances.

[3] Similar to the "cannon" in billiards.

[4] Among some croquet-players, the "push" is considered an undue advantage. It is only an advantage to beginners: as *pushing* a billiard ball might be to an inexperienced billiard-player. Let the beginner have the choice. A "crack" croquet-player will never covet the *push*.

THE ARENA.—The space enclosed within the boundaries of the croquet ground.[5]

THE SPOT.—The point from which the play commences.

THE STARTING STAKE.—The stake from which the play proceeds—placed proximate to the *spot*, at the lower end of the *arena*.

THE TURNING STAKE.—The stake set opposite to the starting stake, and near the upper end of the arena.

THE FOOT.—That part of the arena contiguous to the starting stake.

THE HEAD.—That part of the arena contiguous to the turning stake.

THE FLANKS.—The sides of the rectangle—or of whatever figure may have been chosen for the croquet-ground. They are *right* and *left*. [6]

THE CENTRE.—The central part of the arena.

CENTRAL BRIDGES. — Those in a line between the two stakes. They are *upper*, and *lower*.

FLANK BRIDGES.—Those upon the flanks—also denominated *right* and *left*.

THE FRONT OF A BRIDGE is that side, from which the player must proceed, in passing through or *running* it.

THE BACK OF A BRIDGE.—The side reverse to the *front*. [7]

AN OBLIQUE BRIDGE.—A bridge, the plane of whose arch is not perpendicular to the horizon, or to the *course* of play.

[5] For a fuller explanation of this, and several succeeding phrases, see Chapters II., III., and IV.

[6] Not in reference to the *head* and *foot* of the arena, but to the position of the players—when standing by the starting stake, with their faces turned towards the ground.

[7] The *flank* bridges have but one front : as the ball is required to pass through them only in one direction. The *central* ones, on the contrary, have to be *run* both ways; and their front, at any time, is determined by the ball's position in the game. The *left flank* bridges front towards the *foot* of the ground, the right ones in the opposite direction, or towards its *head*.

A PROPER BRIDGE.—That which the player intends to pass through, is his, or her, *proper* bridge, for the time.

RUNNING A BRIDGE. — When a ball has been driven through the arch of its *proper* bridge, either by a blow of the mallet, by roquet, croquet, ricochet, concussion, or roquet-croquet, it is said to *run* that bridge. [8]

RUEING A BRIDGE.—When a ball, struck by the mallet, fails to reach the bridge at which it has been played, it is said to *rue* it.

OVERRUNNING A BRIDGE.—When a ball struck by the mallet rolls past, and not through, the bridge at which it has been played, it is said to *overrun* it.

TOLLING THE STAKE.—A ball struck *against the turning stake* by mallet, roquet, ricochet, concussion, croquet, or roquet-croquet, at its *proper* time,—that is, after having run the *central* and *left flank* bridges *upward*,— is said to *toll* or *pay toll* to the stake.

STRIKING OUT.—A ball struck against the *starting* stake by mallet, roquet, ricochet, concussion, croquet, or roquet-croquet, after having run *all* the bridges—the central ones in both directions—and tolled the turning stake, is *struck out* : that is, out of the game.

THE GRAND ROUND. — The "grand round" consists in duly running all the bridges—the central ones in both directions—tolling the turning stake in its proper time, and returning to the *spot*—whence the player may either *strike out*, or continue the play.

HALF ROUND.—Having reached the point, where the turning stake is to be tolled.

THE COURSE.—The direction taken by the ball on its round.

POSITION.—A ball is *in position*, when it lies in *front* of its proper bridge, with a possibility of running it by a

[8] As will be found by the "Rules," passing through a bridge in any other way than those mentioned above, is not considered as *running* it.

single blow of the mallet; and *out of position*, when the contrary is the case. [9]

MAKING POSITION.—Making roquet, or ricochet, on a ball already in position.

A FRIEND.—A partner in the game.

AN ENEMY.—An adversary.

A SIDE.—A set of partners, or *friends*.

HELPING A FRIEND.—Roque'ing, or croque'ing a friend's ball into position; causing it to run a bridge, toll the turning stake; or otherwise forwarding it on its round.

SPOILING AN ENEMY.—Striking an enemy's ball out of position, by roquet, croquet, ricochet, concussion, or roquet-croquet, and so retarding it on its round.

ATTACKING.—Playing at an enemy's ball, for the purpose of *spoiling* it.

NURSING.—Croque'ing a ball—either friend or enemy— through, or around, its own proper bridge; then running the bridge; roque'ing and croque'ing the same ball again; and so proceeding on the round. [10]

CLIMBING ON THE SCAPE-GOAT.—Roque'ing a ball into a better position for the player: so that the roque'ing ball may get in front of its own proper bridge, or obtain some other advantage of position.

THE CORNERS.—The points of passage, between the lines of flank and central bridges.

TURNING A CORNER.—Proceeding from the flank to the central bridges, or *vice versâ*; and *running* one or more of both in the same *tour* of play. [11]

A BOOBY.—A ball that has attempted to run the first bridge, and either *rues* or *overruns* it.

A BRIDGED BALL.—A ball that has run the first bridge.

[9] The position is *good* or *bad*, according to the distance and direction of the bridge from the ball.

[10] *Nursing* is a species of play especially provoking to the "enemy."

[11] This can only be accomplished by *climbing on the scape-goat*, or making roquet or ricochet, on a ball already in position.

THE LEADING BALL.—The ball played first from the spot.

A ROVER.—A ball that has made the grand round.

MARSHALLING THE SIDES.—Making the match.

CHIEFS.—The players selected to marshall the sides.

STRIKING FOR FIRST CHOICE.—The chiefs "strike" for first choice of *friends*, by playing a ball at the starting stake, from between the piers of bridge, No. 1; whoever places the ball nearest to the stake has the choice.[12]

A DEAD BALL.—A *rover* struck against the starting stake, and therefore struck out of the game.

VICTORY.—When all of a side succeed in *striking out*.

"UP THE COUNTRY." — A ball croque'd beyond the boundaries is sent to "Hong Kong," or "up the country." The owner, with an indifferent grace stands gazing after it; and the journey, required to bring it back within the arena, is usually performed with an air of the most profound melancholy—not unmingled with chagrin!

---

[12] Equivalent to "stringing" in billiards. The chief who gains the strike has also the option of playing first, or declining to lead, as will be found in THE RULES.

CHAPTER II.

The Ground.

ALMOST any piece of level *lea* land will serve as an *arena* for the play of Croquet.[1]

A *correct* croquet-ground will be a perfectly horizontal plane, without any obliquity or unevenness.[2]

The turf should be of the smoothest that can be obtained, with the grass carefully cut, and the *moss killed out of it.*[3]

The ground should be frequently rolled—and with the heaviest of rollers—until the surface become thoroughly hard and firm.[4]

---

[1] Many people are deterred from entering upon the game of croquet, under the impression, that they have not ground suitable for the play. In most cases this idea is erroneous. There are few cottage dwellings in England, either rural or suburban, that cannot command a croquet-ground,—from having a plot of grass turf already established, or the easy means of making one. By a judicious arrangement of the bridges, croquet may be played upon a piece of ground not larger than the floor of a good-sized dining-room.

[2] If the perfect level is not obtainable, and the surface be oblique, or undulating, the play is still *possible*, though not so *pleasant.* The player will take into calculation the declivities of the ground; and, as this calls forth an extra display of skill, it is questionable whether a croquet-ground of sloping surface may not afford as good sport as one that is horizontal. At all events, both parties to the play will be equally affected by any imperfection of this kind; and therefore neither can have cause to complain of a disadvantage.

[3] The same remark applies to a rough surface, as to one that is sloping. The play is still possible, but not so pleasant.

[4] *Hardness* is one of the essential qualities of a croquet-ground. Where

The ground should be chosen within the precincts of the shrubbery, and not upon the open lawn. [5]

The shape of a croquet-ground,—that is, the *arena*,— should be that of an oblong square or rectangle. [6]

The dimensions of a croquet-ground depend a good deal upon the character of the surface. Where the turf is un-exceptionable, the arena should be a rectangle, of *thirty* yards in length by about *twenty* in breadth. [7]

---

the surface is soft and yielding, either from the nature of the soil, or from being overgrown with moss, not only are the balls impeded in their progress, but that one upon which the foot rests while making the croquet, gets pressed into the ground, so as to make it necessary to take it up, and *dress* the spot, before proceeding with the play.

[5] Croquet is a game of the *parterre* rather than the *pasture;* and as it must needs be frequently played under a hot sun, the shade of the copse should be convenient. In winter too—*for croquet is a game for all seasons*—the shrubbery affords shelter.

The only objection to having the croquet-ground within the shrub-bery, is the difficulty of there finding a sufficient space of grass-grown surface. Some ornamental shrub or tree is too highly prized to be sacrificed—even to the charming game of croquet!

Let such trees stand for the present. The time is not distant, when they will be transplanted, or cut down ruthlessly and without remorse— yea, flung into the fire as faggots—to make way for this sweet pastime —itself to be cherished, as if it were the tree of life!

[6] It is not absolutely *en rigueur* that this should be its shape. The square, circle, or ellipse, will answer equally well—the ellipse even better,—but the rectangular form is preferred, as being the most con-venient.

If the turfed surface be not large enough to admit any of the regular figures, of sufficient size, the arena may be of irregular shape, having for boundaries the edges of walks, borders of flower-beds, &c.

Benches may be placed for the *spectators;* but it should be a grand forfeit for a player to use them. The sedentary *pose* conduces to neglect of the play—a crime not to be tolerated, either in *friend* or *enemy.*

[7] The dimensions given will be found to answer well upon perfectly level ground, where the turf is smooth, and carefully kept. Otherwise, the size of the arena,—as well as the distances between the bridges,—

The boundaries should be marked, either by a slight line traced upon the turf, a trench, or a parapet. [8]

One of the shorter sides of the rectangle becomes the base, and is denominated the *foot*. [9]

The opposite end of the arena is the *head;* and the play is *upward* or *downward,* as it proceeds from the foot to the head, or *vice versâ.*

The sides of the rectangle are the *flanks*—denominated *right* and *left*. [10]

The *corners* of the croquet-ground are the four corners of the rectangular figure forming the arena. [11]

The *centre* is the centre of whatever figure may have been adopted for the arena. If the shape be oval, it is the point midway between the two centres of the ellipse. If a circle, it is the circle's true centre. In a square or

may be reduced. The breadth of a croquet-ground is of much less importance than its length, and admits of greater variation according to circumstances.

[8] If the arena be an irregular figure, or one *improvised* for the occasion, the boundary lines may be *agreed upon* by the players, without being actually traced out. On the other hand, if it be intended to have a permanent croquet-ground (and who is there without such intention?), then its boundary should be marked out by one of the modes suggested. Either the trench or parapet is preferable to the simple line: as both serve to prevent the balls from being driven to an inconvenient distance "up the country." The trench need not be more than a few inches in depth, by eighteen or twenty in breadth; while the parapet—which is a simple embankment of earth—may be turfed, or otherwise made ornamental.

[9] Usually that lying nearest to the dwelling.

[10] In reference to the position of any one standing at the *foot,* and facing towards the arena; when the *right flank* is that to the right hand —the left being, of course, on the opposite side of the ground.

[11] These are not to be mistaken for the "corners" spoken of in the chapter on THE SLANG. The latter are the points of passage from flank to central bridges, and *vice versâ.* A fuller description of them will be found in the chapter on THE ARRANGEMENT.

rectangle, it is the point of intersection of the two diameters; and if the figure be irregular, its centre will be the point of bisection of the straight line lying between the two stakes. [12]

[12] In actual play this point is of no importance. It is altogether imaginary; and is introduced only as an aid to the comprehension of the rules and instructions.

CHAPTER III.

The Croqueterie.

THE implements required for the game of croquet—the "Croqueterie"—are BALLS, MALLETS, BRIDGES, and STAKES.[1]

THE BALLS.—In a complete set of *Croqueterie* there are eight.[2]

They should be perfectly spherical.

The correct size is a circumference of 10 inches; or, if the wood be heavy, still less. Larger than this, the ball becomes an unmanageable affair.

The best wood for a croquet ball is that which is lightest, and at the same time least liable to split. Any of the hard woods—as oak, ash, elm, or beech—will do, provided they be turned *under* a circumference of 10 inches. Otherwise they will be too heavy; for the simple reason that the violent blow, required to propel them over the turf, interferes with the *skill* of the play.

---

[1] Usually termed a "set of croquet things:" a title sufficiently discriminate, but scarce sufficiently technical.

[2] The full set are only used when eight players take part in the game. Four players may also use eight balls, each taking two; but when only four enter the arena, the game will be much better with the like number of balls. As a rule, when there are two or four players, four balls should be taken; when three, or six, six balls; and when eight enter the game, of course, the full number must be used. Croquet does not contemplate five or seven players; though either of these numbers may be admitted, by one of the players taking two balls.

For the same reason boxwood is even less suitable; and lignum-vitæ least of all.[3]

Willow is sufficiently light; but possesses the serious defect of being easily split, and also *dinted* by the blows of the mallet.

Sycamore (*Acer pseudo-platanus*) is of the proper specific gravity; and, provided it be the *heart*-wood of an old tree, and not the *sap*-wood of a young one, will be found the best material for a croquet-ball. It is liable to get *dinted*, like the willow; but if not *abused*—that is, struck with too much violence, until it has become *hardened* to the play— the marks will be made regularly all over it, and it will in time recover its original rotundity.

Sap-wood of chestnut is nearly, if not quite, equal to the sycamore; and either one or the other may be depended upon, as a proper material for a croquet-ball.

Let your balls, then, be of sycamore, or light chestnut— each exactly 10 inches in circumference.

Paint them of as many colours as there are balls. The more vivid the colour, the prettier will be the effect on the green sward, and the pleasanter the play.[4]

The balls are designated by their respective colours: as

[3] Hitherto, large boxwood balls have been the most *fashionable;* for what reason it is difficult to say. They are simply a stupid monstrosity —no more adapted to the game of croquet, than a ball of gold, or a ten-pound shot, to the play of billiards. Their presence upon the croquet-ground may, perhaps, be explained by their superior beauty— a little, perhaps, by the superior *profit* arising from their *sale;*—but more than all, by an utter innocence of all knowledge of the game on the part of the *toy-makers,* who have introduced them.

[4] The painted balls are, perhaps, quite as pretty as those, either of boxwood or lignum-vitæ,—especially after these have been some time in use, and have lost their shining surface. Objections may be made to the paint, as liable to *flake* off. If properly laid on, it will last a long time; moreover, nothing is easier than to renew it.

red, blue, green, &c.; and the player of each adopts the designation of the ball.[5]

The Mallets, like the balls, are eight in number.[6]

It is essential to have them of a particular size and shape—both as to the *head* and *shank.*

The *head* should be 4 inches in length, and cylindrical—though not an exact cylinder, but rather of the shape of a dice-box.

At either end it should have a circumference of 7 inches, exactly; and the ends should be slightly convex on their facings.[7]

The mallet-head should proceed from the lathe of the turner; and may be ornamented by circular lines traced out with the chisel; but these should be sparingly used.

The *shank* should also be turned; and of just that thickness to be conveniently grasped by the delicate fingers of a lady. It should be slightly rounded off at the upper end; and decrease gradually in diameter, to its point of insertion into the head. A circumference of $2\frac{3}{4}$ inches at the *handle,* is a proper thickness for a mallet-shank. It may also be ornamented by circular tracings; but these should be of the slightest; and all deep flutings, or inequalities, are to be avoided.[8]

[5] This is a very convenient practice: since a match at croquet is often played by people—not only *thitherto,* but *thenceforth*—strangers to each other.

[6] This number is even less absolute for the mallets, than for the balls. In a case of *dire* necessity, a less number would suffice; but for convenience, it is proper that each player be provided with a mallet.

[7] Some prefer the facings *flat.* A compromise may be effected by having one end flat, and the other convex; though this fashion will interfere with the true balance of the implement.

[8] Croquet mallets are generally seen with a few inches of the shank painted, at the point of its junction with the head. The design is, that each player should use a mallet, corresponding to the colour of

The shank of the mallet should be perfectly straight : as without this a true blow cannot be given. In fact, *straightness* is a quality as essential to a croquet mallet, as to a billiard cue. A crooked stick should be plucked out, and replaced by a true one.

The *length* of the mallet is a matter of importance. It should be (head and shank measured together) exactly 2 feet 6 inches. Even shorter than this may be used with advantage; but, if longer, the upper end will be found an impediment—by its coming in contact with the arm of the player, and thus destroying both the aim and impetus of the blow.[9]

The wood out of which the mallets are to be made must have *weight*—the very opposite quality to that required by the balls. In fact, the weight of the former should be in proportion to that of the latter — not inversely, but direct. A heavy ball will require a heavy mallet to propel it; and the converse is equally true.

Both head and shank of the mallet may be made out of the same sort of timber; or they may be of two different kinds. Ash, though not an elegant, is an excellent

the ball. The idea is ingenious, but idle; and something worse: since it is a source of trouble in the distribution of the implements, not unfrequently leading to confusion. The identification of the mallets—after they have been once appropriated by the respective players—is of no consequence whatever.

[9] Most of the mallets in use. are much larger than the dimensions above given. Those who manufacture them are evidently unacquainted with the game of croquet. It only needs running through a single *round*, to become convinced of the superiority of the short-shanked mallets. Those in possession of the *long shanks* may easily have them *razeed*—by simply plucking them out, sawing off the requisite number of inches from the smaller end, and restoring them to the socket. A similar hint may be given about balls, that are found too large. Take them to the village turner; and let him reduce them to *ten inches* in circumference: though perhaps a new set may be as cheap, and better.

wood for either—possessing the necessary requisites of *weight, strength*, and *toughness*. Box may be used, by those who prefer a more polished implement: since its great weight—the very quality which renders this wood ill-fitted for the ball—adapts it to the mallet.[10]

THE BRIDGES. — There are *ten* bridges to a set of croqueterie.[11]

They are simple constructions; and may be *built* by any one. They consist of pieces of iron rod, sharpened at both ends, and bent into the shape of an arch.

At each end, six or eight inches of the rod should be left straight—to form the *piers* of the arch when the bridge is *erected*. This is done, by inserting the sharpened ends into the turf, and driving them in firmly.

A rod of three feet in length will form a proper bridge—giving a span of about twelve inches.[12]

The iron rod, of which the bridges are made, may either be round or square; but it should be of sufficient thickness, to guard against being broken or twisted out of shape when trodden upon. Strong wire is sometimes used for the construction of the bridges; but it is still more subject

[10] If boxwood mallets be used, the dimensions above given must be strictly adhered to: else they will be altogether too unwieldy. Those at present accompanying the boxwood balls are, like the latter, by far too heavy, — each being quite a *load* for a lady to carry across the croquet-ground.

Beechwood shanks, much used in the cheaper sets of croqueterie, are worthless at any price. This wood will do well enough for the head; but as a shank it is certain to become *warped*—a defect, under all circumstances, to be shunned.

[11] There may be twelve, or even more; but ten is the number usually *erected;* and ten are sufficient.

[12] Should the croquet-ground be a small one—having a smooth well-kept surface—the span of the arch may be less than twelve inches. The reduction can be easily effected: by bending the ends of the iron rod inward, before inserting them into the turf. *This* may be done to advantage on any ground—where the bridges are found too easy to *run.*

to the drawback mentioned. Round rod iron, of three-eighths or three-tenths of an inch in diameter, will be found to answer admirably.[13]

THE STAKES.—The stakes are two in number—respectively denominated the *starting* and *turning* stake.

It is of no importance what sort of material they are made of—whether wood, or iron.

They should be about the thickness of a mallet shank; if of wood, turned in the lathe; and sharpened at one end—so as to be easily driven into the turf. They should not be over two feet in length; as when standing *taller*, they may interfere with the action of the players.

The *starting* stake should have eight rings painted around it—their edges contiguous to each other; and all of different colours—corresponding to the colours of the eight balls.[14]

It will be a further advantage to have the *turning* stake painted in a similar fashion; but care must be taken that the succession of colours be the same on both.[15]

---

[13] In the more costly sets of "croqueterie" the bridges are usually of bronze, or simply *bronzed*. Others are of black iron rod—which might be made prettier by painting. A still better plan has been adopted by one of the manufacturers—that is, painting the bridges of different colours, so that *no two of them are alike*. This is an excellent idea: as the colour upon the bridges will be found to act as *an aid to the memory, in recording the positions of the players.*

[14] These rings are required as *remembrancers*: to prompt the players to the proper time for taking their *tour* of play. The ring, which stands highest on the stake, proclaims that the ball of that colour is to be played first; the next below calls for the ball of its colour; and so on in succession. Thus when any ball has finished its *tour*, the one which *should* follow may be at once told: by glancing at the *Jacob's rod.*

[15] In some sets of croqueterie which we have seen, the rings are also painted on the mallet shanks—near the point of insertion with the head: so that the player, no matter how distant he may be from the stakes, may always *tell* the order of succession, by simply glancing at the mallet.

Such, then, are the implements of the game—yclept the "Croqueterie."[16]

Before closing this chapter, a special remark is required upon the subject of the *croqueterie*.

It is not too much to say: that half the pleasure of the game consists *in playing it with proper implements*.

There is an *idiosyncrasy* (if we may .be allowed the expression) in croquet balls and mallets — a positive necessity as to size, shape, and weight,—just as there is in the cue and ball for billiards, or the bat and ball of the cricket-ground; and every departure from the correct standard detracts from the interest of the game.

Many incipient players of croquet,—who might otherwise have imbibed a *passion* for this pastime— have had their interest chilled into indifference, even to forsaking it altogether, for no other reason, than that of having been provided with implements unsuited to its play.[17]

---

[16] *Croquet markers* are sometimes employed, to record the positions of the players. There are several kinds of these "inventions," all alike useless—all equally calculated to create confusion. The oft-repeated manipulation of these markers becomes a tiresome necessity. Besides, it is just as easy to recollect the situation of the ball, as to attend to the *shifting* of the marker; and perhaps *a trifle easier*.

A croquet player, who takes any interest in the game, will remember the position of the ball—especially if provided with the painted bridges mentioned in a preceding note.

[17] The *cheapest* sets of "croquet things,"—that is, those sold at the lowest prices,—are certainly the best: rather an anomaly in the economy of manufactures. The reason is, that they are of smaller size, and usually made of more suitable materials. By far the best we have yet seen, are those in which the mallets are branded with a star, and the name "Bernard & Co." They are the nearest of any to the correct weight, shape, and size; and are those spoken of, as having the bridges painted of different colours, and the ringed arrangement on the shanks of the mallets.

With the huge, unwieldy *weapons,* now in general use, a *true scientific stroke* is impossible. So, too, is the carrying out of any of those cunning *combinations,* that form the *intellectuality* of the play, and in which the game of croquet is specially abundant—in such points, certainly not yielding to billiards, and, perhaps, not even to chess.[18]

[18] It is not uncommon, upon the croquet-ground, to hear a preference expressed for *large* and *heavy* balls. Any individual so declaring him or herself, may be *safely* set down as a "gringe" in the game of croquet.

CHAPTER IV.

The Arrangement.

THE arena having been chosen, and its boundaries marked out, it remains only to set the stakes and bridges.[1]

The former are to be considered first.

The position of the *starting* stake will be within the arena, at least 10 feet from that boundary constituting its base or *foot*, and midway between the *flanks*.

The *turning* stake holds a similar relative position to the *head* of the arena: that is, midway between the flanks, and at least 10 feet from the *head*.[2]

The stakes once planted, the positions of the bridges can be determined without much trouble.

---

[1] Once properly placed, it is better to leave them so, than risk an irregular arrangement—by taking them up for the mere purpose of *housing* them. Both stakes and bridges will stand exposure. Both *should be firmly set*, to withstand any collision of the balls.

Hitherto, the arrangement of the bridges has been subject, a good deal to caprice, and a great deal to misconception. It is true, that many modes may be adopted, and still the game of croquet will retain most of its peculiar charms. For the sake of variety, or novelty, an occasional change may be admitted; but the original arrangement will be found the best; and any permanent departure from it must be regarded in the light of a retrograde radicalism.

[2] The distance of the stakes, from the head and foot boundaries, is a point of great importance—though one that is generally disregarded. A ball passing over the boundary, by the rules of the game, can be brought back within the arena. Should this occur in the proximity of either stake—when set close to the boundary line—the ball thus returned, may obtain an advantage not due to the skill of the player— a circumstance ever to be shunned.

The *central* ones—which are Nos. 1, 2, and 6, 7—should be in a line : that is, the straight line lying between the stakes—with their planes perpendicular to it.[3]

Their distances from the stakes, and from each other should be as follows :—No. 1, 10 feet from the starting-stake ; No. 2, a like distance from No. 1 ; while 7 and 6 should be respectively 10 feet and 20 feet from the turning stake.

The distance between 2 and 6 remains indefinite ; and will be greater, or less, according to the length of the arena.[4]

The *flank* bridges are ruled by those of the centre. Nos. 3 and 10 should be in the same *plane* with No. 2 ; one on each flank — at equal distances from it — and midway between it and the side boundaries of the arena.[5]

Bridges 5 and 8 should be in the same plane with No. 6 —one upon each flank, and at the same distance from it as 3 and 10 are from 2. This will bring 3 in the same longitudinal line with 5, and 8 with 10.

A bridge placed midway between each pair of the latter

[3] If it be desired to place them *very* exact, a ready method will be obtained by stretching a piece of string between the two stakes, and planting the bridges over it.

[4] In a croquet-ground of 30 yards long, with the measurements as above, the distance between bridges 2 and 6 would be 30 feet. Where the ground is less than 30 yards in length, of course the distance becomes reduced ; but it is desirable to have bridges 2 and 6 as far apart as possible. The end may be obtained, by setting the other bridges a little closer, or placing the stakes nearer to the boundary lines.

[5] This is supposing the arena to have a breadth of 20 yards—in which case the line of the flank bridges will be 15 feet from that of the central ones. If the ground be narrow, then it will be necessary to place the flank bridges nearer to the boundary lines : as it is desirable to have them as distant as possible from the central ones. It is also of importance that they should not approach too near to the boundaries : hence the advantage of having the arena at least 20 yards in width—or wider, if the ground will admit of it.

will complete the *arrangement*. These last will be Nos. 4 and 9; and they will be in the same plane with each other.[6]

The bridges and stakes having been set in the manner described, there are four points that deserve especial mention. They are the *corners* ; so called, not in reference to the figure of the ground, but to the *round* of play. They are the points of *passage*, from the central to the flank bridges, and *vice versâ*.

There are four of them : — the first lying between bridges 2 and 3 ; the second between 5 and 6; the third between 6 and 8; and the fourth and last between bridges 10 and 2.[7]

The *Spot*, though first regarded in the game—as the point from which the play takes its departure—is the last to be determined in the arrangement. It is a point in the line, between the starting stake and bridge No. 1—one mallet's length from the former. It needs no further definition.[8]

---

[6] The space between each pair of the flank bridges being ruled by the distance from Nos. 2 to 6—of which it is the half—is, like the latter, indefinite. It is of no consequence that there should be an exact amount of feet between each two, so long as they are *sufficiently* apart.

[7] In the arrangement set forth in the scant systems of " Rules" propounded by the toy-makers, there are no *corners*. The upper and lower flank bridges—instead of being respectively in the planes of the inner central ones—are so placed that it is possible, during the same tour of play, to proceed from one line and *through* the other without " climbing the scape-goat," or the intervention of any other advantage.

As the *turning of the corners* is, in truth, one of the most ingenious contrivances of the game of croquet—its performance a feat of genuine skill—it will easily be perceived, that the plan laid down must be, so far, superior to any other.

[8] The Spot may be either marked out on the turf, or left to measurement. Hence the advantage of determining it at one mallet's length from the stake : since this implement—always ready in the hands of the player—can be easily applied to the ground. There is a "rule" in common use, which places the spot 12 *inches* from the starting stake. The sapient propounder of this regulation could never have played the first stroke in a game of croquet ; or, doing so, he must have *pushed* his ball !

CHAPTER V.

The Programme.

THE arrangement—we may term it the *mise en scène*—having been accomplished,.let us look over the *programme* of the play.

The game of croquet is open to any number of players, up to eight. Even ten or twelve *might* take part in it, by using extra balls. The *rules* of the game, in all cases, remain the same; but the interest of the play will vary according to the number of players, and in a kind of inverse ratio—diminishing as the latter is increased. A match of more than eight would prolong the play, beyond —what might be termed—a "reasonable time."[1]

When eight players enter the lists, it is usual to play as *friends*, four and four to a side; but the arrangement of four sets or *sides*, of two friends each, is equally admissible.

Seven players may go through the game, as if there were eight: by some one of either side taking the extra ball, and playing it in its proper tour.[2]

When six enter, the play may be arranged either into two sides of three, or three of two: each player, as in the game of eight, taking a single ball.

If there be only five players upon the ground, the odd

---

[1] A game of eight players is sufficiently *tedious*. With ten or twelve it would be *intolerable*.

[2] Many prefer the game of eight on account of the "company;" but these are not zealous players. With them croquet is only a *pastime*—not a *passion*.

one may be admitted, by the introduction of an extra ball, as above directed—thus constituting a set of six.[3]

The *game of four* may be played with eight balls—each player taking an extra ball, and playing it in its proper *tour*. It is then simply the game of eight; and, like the latter, may be arranged into two sides of four, or four of two.[4]

Three players may either play the game of four—by one of them taking the extra ball—or of six, by each taking two balls.

When there are only two players upon the ground, it becomes simply a game of four—each taking two balls, and playing them alternately.[5]

---

[3] The game of six is much prized by many players. It has the advantage over that of eight—in being more speedily got through with. Besides, the recurrence of each individual's tour of play is more rapid, and the interval of inaction less trying to the patience.

[4] Four players, each on his own account—unless by taking two balls apiece—cannot play the game of croquet in a proper manner. One of the players, unwatched by the rest, may "steal" out, and bring the play to an unexpected ending; or, one may be made the victim of a combination of the other three, and so retarded in his course, that the most indifferent player of the party becomes the winner.

When four enter, they should play two and two, each with a single ball; or, if it be desired to try the individual skill of the players, two balls each may be taken.

The game of four players, each with a single ball, and two and two to a side, is that most relished by zealous croquet-players. It ensures sufficient shortness, and furthermore provides against that irksome impatience, arising from a too long interval between the tours of play.

[5] There is a croquet-player of still more zealous inclinings, who prefers this game to all others. To him a game with six players, or even four, is a tedious trial — slow as the tread of a tortoise. Half crazed about croquet, he is never easy in mind, with his mallet at rest—perfectly happy when that implement is in action, cracking away at his own ball, or croque'ing that of his *enemy*. *Enemies* he rarely has. He does not want them. A single competitor is his choice—the passion of his soul a *good* game of croquet. What to him is the company—players or spectators? What to him are pretty feet,

Whatever be the number of players, the object of each is to make the *grand round*, and ·*strike out* against the starting stake—by the accomplishment of which feat, the "victory" is obtained.[6]

The *course* of the ball in making the grand round is, first, from the spot, through bridges 1 and 2 *upwards*; then to the left flank in front of 3; thence through 3, 4, and 5; thence back to the line of ·the centre in front of 6; thence through 6 and 7, making the *half-round*.

The stake is next *tolled*; after which the ball runs back through 7 and 6, *downwards*, or in a direction contrary to its previous course.

Having re-run 7 and 6, it crosses over to front of the right flank bridges—their front being the reverse to that of those on the left. It then *runs* 8, 9, and 10, *downwards*; crosses again to the centre line above 2; and re-runs 2 and 1 towards the starting stake.

It has thus completed the *grand round*; and, being once more placed upon the *spot*, has the option—either of *striking out*, or continuing the play, with the privileges of the *Rover*.[7]

or provoking ankles? Nothing, or only a vexatious obstruction to his enjoyment of the play! A game of croquet—a *good* game—*with two players, and four balls*—is with him the *ne plus ultra* of sub-solary enjoyment!

Perhaps this selfish fellow may be right. Perhaps the play of croquet—like some other pastimes—may be pleasantest as a *jeu de deux!*

[6] As the victory is not declared, till *all* the friends of a side are struck out, the act of *striking out* is usually delayed by each, until the last of that side has completed the grand round. The striking out of any individual ball—while any of its *friends* are still far back in the game—is a serious loss, instead of a gain, to the *side* to which it belongs: more especially since the *rover* is endowed with certain privileges, which render him either a valuable friend, or a formidable enemy.

[7] Under certain circumstances it is not impossible to make the grand round in a *single tour* of play; but the individual, who can accomplish this feat, may be regarded as a "crack croquet player." An ordinary player will take a dozen—perhaps a score—of

Before entering upon a game of croquet, there are certain preliminary points that deserve attention. Of these the most important is *making the match.*[8]

Out of the company intended to take part in the play, two *chiefs* should be chosen.[9]

Each chief takes a ball,—any ball,—places it between the piers of bridge No. 1 ; and, with a blow of the mallet,

tours to return to the starting-stake; and even a good "hand" at at croquet, will usually require a considerable number, to enable him to accomplish the desired end.

A ball in going its round meets with two distinct classes of interruptions —one voluntary, the other unavoidable. Of the former kind, there is the diverging from its course to attack an *enemy*, by roquet and croquet, and *spoil* the latter's position; or, by the same means, to *help on a friend*. A ball may also voluntarily diverge from its course to *place itself near* a friend, so that the latter, when its tour comes on, may by roque'ing upon it, make position.

The *involuntary* obstructions to the course of a ball are of various kinds:—attempting the bridges, and failing to attain them; passing without *running* them; crossing at the *corners*, without the possibility of *turning* them; being roque'd or croque'd out of position; played out of its proper tour, and duly challenged; attempting to make a roquet, and failing in the attempt; or permitted to "flinch" from under the foot of its player while in the act of croquet;—any of these contingencies will obstruct a ball on its *round*.

[8] This might seem easy of accomplishment. In reality it is not so. Where eight persons enter the arena—some of them being accomplished croquet-players, while others are entirely unacquainted with the game — it is of importance that they should be *marshalled* in such manner, as to make the two *sides* equal, or as near it as may be. To accomplish this, something more than chance must be trusted to; and it is believed that the plan here put forward will conveniently answer the purpose.

[9] Where it is intended to have more than two *sides* in the game, there will be a chief for every side or set of partners. The choice of chiefs may be made by *general consent*—usually falling upon the two most noted players: though this is a point of no importance whatever. The *rôle* of the chiefs is simply to "strike" for the choice of partners; and may be performed by any player, whether a lady or gentleman. After the first tour of play, the chief is no longer distinguished from his or *her* followers.

drives it in the direction of the starting stake—the object being to *lay* it as near as possible to the foot of the stake.

The other chief "strikes" in like fashion; and when the operation is over, the ball that *lies nearest to the stake* wins the right to first choice of friends,—as also the option to lead off in the play.[10]

The chief, who has thus obtained first choice out of the company, names a friend; but *only one at a time.* The adversary has second choice, and also selects a friend. The third choice belongs to the victorious chief; the fourth to the adversary; and so on, till the *sides* are selected—when the match is considered *made.*

The chief, who leads the play, will now take up that ball, whose colour is represented by the ring standing highest on the stake, and one of the mallets — any one.[11]

The adversary must take the ball whose colour comes next; the third falls to the friend first chosen; the fourth to the friend chosen by the adversary; and so on in alternate succession of friends and enemies, till all the balls have been appropriated.[12]

Each player being provided with a ball and mallet, the

[10] It is of little importance which chief "strikes" first. The first has the advantage of placing his ball in the other's way; while the second has the chance of *striking it out of the way*, and so getting nearest to the stake. If there be any dispute, as to who should strike first, it may be settled by using only one ball, and marking the spot where the first player may have succeeded in placing it.

[11] It is of no importance that the painting on the shank of the mallet should correspond to the colour of the ball. As observed in the chapter "Croqueterie," this *ingenious idea* often begets confusion.

In appropriating the mallets, each player will endeavour to get hold of the one that is lightest; but in the "stock" of croqueterie to be met with on most lawns, a mallet of sufficient lightness will be sought for in vain.

[12] If there be only four players, or four balls, it will not be absolutely necessary to look to the rings upon the stake. They are merely

game may begin—the play proceeding in the order of
the coloured rings upon the stake, *from the top downwards.*[13]

intended as *prompters;* when, with a large number of players, it is
difficult to tell "whose tour comes next." Even with only four
in the game, they may be occasionally glanced at with advantage:
more especially when the heavy forfeit for *misplay* is taken into
consideration.

[13] It will still further simplify the process of entering upon the game,
if the players appropriate the balls falling to the lot of each, *at the
time when the choice of friends is being made.*

CHAPTER VI.

THE RULES.

The Start.

1. THE *chief* who has won the first choice of *friends*, has the right to lead off the play.[1]

2. The hostile chief plays next.[2]

3. The others enter upon the game, in the order in which they were *marshalled* by their respective chiefs,—friends and enemies playing alternately.

4. Each ball must first be played from the *Spot*.

5. The stroke of the ball may be either a *push*, or a *blow*; but *only one hand* is to be used in making it.[3]

6. Each ball continues its play, so long as it succeeds in *making a point* in the game; and terminates it, on the failure to do so.[4]

[1] The first chief may resign this right by courtesy, or require the other chief to lead off, or they may strike again for first play; but as this often conducts to a re-distribution of the balls, and some consequent confusion, it will be better to adhere to the rule.

[2] This is supposing two sides, and therefore only two chiefs in the game. If there be more, the chiefs follow in the order of their "strike."

[3] The stroke of the mallet is delivered whenever it moves the ball—no matter how short the distance the latter may have been driven. Objections are made to pushing the ball, and the "Rules" of the toy-makers are against it; though in truth it is the absurdly heavy mallet of these same toy-makers that renders pushing a necessity. It is only an advantage to the tyro, or the indifferent player. Except when obstructed by a bridge, stake, or otherwise, an experienced "player" will no more think of *pushing* the ball, than a "crack" billiard-player would of using the butt end of his cue.

[4] For the continuance, or termination, of a *tour of play*, see "Rules," under this heading.

The Booby.

7. A booby cannot croquet another booby.

8. A booby cannot croquet a *bridged* ball.

9. A booby cannot be croque'd by a bridged ball.

10. A booby may *displace* another booby or a bridged ball by roquet, ricochet, or concussion.　•

11. A bridged ball may displace a booby by roquet, ricochet, or concussion.

12. If a booby be driven through the first bridge by roquet, ricochet, or concussion, either of another booby or a bridged ball, it becomes a *bridged* ball.

13. If a booby bridge another booby, and at the same blow succeed in running the first bridge, it may again roquet the ball it has bridged, croquet it, and continue.[5]

14. If a bridged ball succeed in bridging a booby, it may again make roquet, or ricochet upon it, and *then* croquet it.[6]

The Bridges.

15. If a bridge be obliqued—either to the line of the *course*, or the plane of the horizon—any player may restore it to the perpendicular.[7]

16. No player may oblique a bridge, standing perpendicular ; nor change it from one oblique to another.

17. If a bridge be accidentally displaced by a stroke of the mallet, the foot of the player, the concussion of a ball,

[5] Of course, after running the bridge, both boobies become bridged balls, and subject to the laws for continuance and termination of *tour*—which see. Throughout the " Rules," a ball, not specified as a *booby*, is understood to mean a ball that has been bridged.

[6] It cannot croquet from the roquet, or ricochet, which passed the booby through the bridge : since either must have been made before the booby became a bridged ball, and therefore before it became liable to the croquet.

[7] The proper position of a bridge is perpendicular to the plane of the horizon, with its own plane perpendicular to the line of the *course*. (See Chap. IV.)

or otherwise, it is to be restored to its position without forfeit.

Running the Bridges.

18. A bridge can be *run* only by a direct blow of the mallet, by roquet, croquet, ricochet, concussion, or roquet-croquet.

19. If a ball proceeding from a direct blow of the mallet, or otherwise, strike against a bridge, stake, or other obstacle, and rebound through its *proper* bridge in the direction of the *course*, it *runs* it.[8]

20. If a ball, after running a bridge, strike an obstacle, and recoil back through the bridge, the *run* remains good.

21. A bridge is not *run*, unless the ball passes *clear through*—so that no part of it remain under the arch.[9]

22. A ball resting under the arch of a bridge is *in position* for that bridge, if it have been driven between the piers *from the front*, or in the direction of the course.

23. A ball resting under the arch of a bridge is *not in position* for that bridge, if it have been driven between the piers from *the reverse side*, or placed under the arch by *hand*, for the purpose of making croquet.[10]

[8] Should the obstacle struck, however, be the person of one of the players, the *run* will only hold good at the option of the *enemy:* that is, the enemy of the player causing the accident.

[9] It is often a debatable question, as to *when* a ball is "through" the bridge. By good fortune the question is easily solved, and by the simplest of methods. Place the shank of the mallet against the two piers of the bridge, *in front;* and if the ball be not through, even by the hundredth part of an inch, the deficiency will declare itself. If the bridge be obliqued, either the owner of the ball, or the enemy, has the right to restore it to the perpendicular.

[10] In either case, the test described in Note 9, will be effectual. If the ball be doubtfully under the arch of the bridge, and *in position*, the mallet-shank is to be applied in *front* of the piers; while, if doubtfully *not in position*, the shank is to be laid along the *reverse* side.

24. A ball passing through its *proper* bridge from the *reverse* side, or in a direction contrary to its course, makes no *point* in the game.

25. If a ball, in executing the croquet, flinch from under the foot of the player, and pass through its proper bridge in the direction of the course, it does not *run* the bridge.

26. A ball passing through any bridge, other than its proper one, in any direction, makes no point.

27. A ball, striking, or struck, against the piers of a bridge, makes no point.

28. A ball may run two or more bridges by a blow of the mallet, by roquet, croquet, ricochet, concussion, or roquet-croquet.[11]

The Stakes.

29. If either of the stakes be obliqued to the plane of the horizon, any player at any time may restore it to the perpendicular.

30. No player may oblique a stake standing perpendicular; nor change one oblique to another.

31. The *turning stake* may be *tolled*, by a ball proceeding from a direct blow of the mallet, from a roquet, a croquet, a ricochet, a concussion, or a roquet-croquet.

32. If a ball, in executing the croquet, flinch from under the foot of the player, and strike the turning stake, even at its proper time for tolling it, it does not *toll* the stake.

33. The turning stake can only be *tolled*, by a ball that has completed the *half-round*.

34. If a ball, after making the half-round, strike the

---

[11] For running two or more bridges, by a direct blow of the mallet, there are *rewards*. See *Double Points*.

turning stake by rebound from a bridge, another ball, or any *fixed* obstacle of the ground, it *tolls* the stake.[12]

35. The slightest perceptible touch constitutes a *tolling* of the stake.

36. A ball may run one or more bridges, and toll the turning stake—or *vice versâ*—by a single blow of the mallet, by roquet, croquet, ricochet, concussion, or roquet-croquet.

37. A ball, having made the *grand round*, may be struck *out* against the starting stake, by a direct blow of the mallet, by roquet, croquet, ricochet, concussion, roquet-croquet, or by a *flinch* from under the foot of the player while executing the croquet.[13]

38. If a ball, having made the grand round, strike the starting stake by rebound from a bridge, another ball or any *fixed* obstacle of the ground, it is *struck out* of the game.[14]

39. A ball may run one or more bridges, and be *struck out* at the same blow.

40. A ball striking, or struck, against the turning stake, at any other time than when *tolling* it, makes no point in the game.

41. A ball striking, or struck, against the starting stake, before completing the grand round, makes no point in the game.

The Roquet.

42. A ball can roquet another by a direct blow of the

---

[12] Should the obstacle causing the rebound be the person of one of the players, it is at the option of the enemy of this player, whether the *tolling* may hold good.

[13] In this case the enemy, who has the option, decides for the striking out; since the point is a disadvantage to the unfortunate *flincher*.

[14] As in the case of running a bridge, and tolling the turning stake, should the accident be caused by one of the players, it is the *enemy* of that player who has the option of deciding.

mallet, or proceeding from the mallet by rebound from a bridge, a stake, or other *fixed* obstacle of the ground.[15]

43. The slightest perceptible contact, between the two balls, constitutes a *roquet*.

44. A ball having roque'd another, may strike it again without any intervening play; but the second contact does not constitute a roquet.

45. If a ball, after roque'ing another, run one or more bridges, or toll the turning stake, it may again make roquet upon the same ball.

46. A ball, that has been roque'd, remains on the spot to which it has rolled—subject to further displacement by croquet.

47. If a ball, in the execution of the croquet, *flinch* from under the foot of the player and strike another ball, the contact does not constitute a roquet.

The Ricochet.

48. *Ricochet* can be made only by a ball, that has already roque'd or ricoche'd upon another.[16]

49. The slightest perceptible contact between the playing ball and that played upon, constitutes a *ricochet*.

50. A ball having ricoche'd upon another, may strike it again without any intervening play; but the second contact does not constitute a ricochet.

51. If a ball after ricoche'ing upon another, run one or more bridges, or toll the turning-stake, it may again make ricochet on the same ball.

52. A ricoche'd ball remains on the spot to which it has rolled—subject to further displacement by croquet.

[15] If the rebound be from the person of a player, the enemy can decide against the roquet.

[16] The ricochet is simply a double roquet. It may be triple or quadruple, according to the number of balls touched by the playing one.

Concussion.

53. A ball diplaced by *concussion*, remains on the spot to which it has rolled—not subject to further displacement by croquet.

The Croquet.

54. A ball can only croquet another, on which it has made roquet or ricochet.

55. A ball, having made roquet, may decline the croquet.

56. A ball having made roquet—and declined the croquet—may continue its play, either from the spot into which it has rolled after the roquet, or from the side of the roque'd ball.[17]

57. A ball having made ricochet on several balls, may croquet all, or any, of them.

58. A series of ricoche'd balls must be croque'd, in the order in which they have been touched.

59. A ball having made ricochet, can decline to croquet all the ricoche'd balls, and continue its tour of play either from the spot into which it has rolled after the ricochet, or from the side of any one of the balls ricoche'd.[18]

60. A ball having made ricochet, can decline to croquet any of the ricoche'd balls; and croquet any other, or others, of them.

61. A ball having croque'd a ricoche'd ball, cannot go back to one previously touched in the same ricochet; but must continue its tour, by playing from the place where

[17] With some, the rule is: if the croquet be declined, to compel continuance from the spot, into which the playing ball has rolled after the roquet. Altogether irrational: since the playing ball may place itself contiguous to that roque'd; *sham* the croquet by the slightest blow; and then proceed from the coveted place.

[18] To deprive it of this privilege, would be equally irrational with the rule referred to in Note 17.

it has made the croquet, or else proceed to the ball ricoche'd next in order, croquet this, or play from its side; or declining this croquet, proceed to the next; and so on, to the end of the series.[19]

62. If a ball, after making roquet or ricochet, has been taken up from the ground, it must continue its tour of play, either from the side of the roque'd or ricoche'd ball, by croquet or otherwise.

63. A ball may croquet every other ball in the game—whether friend or enemy—*once between the running of every two bridges.*

64. A ball may croquet every other ball in the game—whether friend or enemy—*once between the running of a bridge, and the tolling of the turning stake; or vice versâ.*

65. A ball having croque'd another, cannot croquet it a second time, during the same tour of play, without running a bridge, or tolling the turning stake.

66. A croquet is completed, when the mallet makes a perceptible—that is, an *audible*—blow against the croque'ing ball—whether that to be croque'd stir from its place or not.

67. If the mallet altogether miss the croque'ing ball, the croquet is still incomplete; and the blow may be repeated.

68. If a ball roquet another, and at the same blow run a bridge, it may either proceed to croquet the roque'd ball; or decline, and again make roquet upon it, before taking the croquet.

69. If a ball roquet another, and at the same time toll the turning stake, it may either proceed to croquet the roque'd ball, or decline, and again make roquet upon it, before taking the croquet.

The Roquet-Croquet.

70. Roquet-croquet is the peculiar privilege of the

[19] A ricochet on more than two balls, is a rare *fluke;* but the rule is thus extended, in order to meet every possible eventuality.

Rover; and may only be executed by a ball that has completed the *grand round.*[20]

71. The rover can roquet-croquet all the other balls in the game—whether friends or enemies—*but only once during the same tour of play.*

The Tour of Play.

72. A ball may continue its *tour* of play, after each successful stroke, or *point,* made in the game.[21]

73. Running a bridge entitles to continuance of tour.

74. Tolling the stake entitles continuance of tour.

75. The tour is continued after making a roquet or ricochet.

76. The tour continues after a croquet.

77. After roquet-croquet, the rover continues its tour.

78. The tour *terminates,* on the failure of the playing-ball to make a successful stroke, or *point,* in the game.

79. A ball striking another ball, after having roque'd it, and without any intervening play, terminates its tour.[22]

80. A ball striking another ball, after having ricoche'd

[20] It is given exclusively to the rover, as a compensation for the loss of other privileges—which the latter must abandon on becoming a rover: such as the right to re-croquet after running a bridge, or tolling the stake. Also for the risk the rover ball constantly runs, of being *struck out.*

Roquet-croquet is, moreover, a *premium to prowess.*

On some croquet-grounds the roquet-croquet, or "taking two turns," is allowed to every bridged ball; and there are players who prefer this fashion. A better knowledge of the game will teach such players, that with every ball using the roquet-croquet, the game *skilfully* played might be prolonged for a lifetime.

[21] It must be a *point* made by the playing ball itself, not by one on which it has played: such as the latter running a bridge by roquet, ricochet, concussion, or otherwise.

[22] When the *tour* is said to *terminate,* by any of the contingencies mentioned in the "Rules," it is under the supposition that the playing ball, at the same blow, makes no other point that entitles it to continue.

upon it, and without any intervening play, terminates its tour.

81. A ball striking another ball, after having croque'd it, and without any intervening play, terminates its tour.

82. A ball failing either to run a bridge, make roquet, or ricochet upon another ball, or toll the turning stake, terminates its tour.

83. Making roquet on a booby terminates the tour.

84. The tour of a booby terminates with a single blow—unless the blow make it a bridged ball.

85. If a ball declining the croquet, and playing from the side of the roque'd ball, displace the latter, the tour of the playing ball terminates.

86. If the rover, in executing the roquet-croquet, does not displace the other ball, the blow terminates its tour.[23]

87. If the rover has made either roquet, croquet, ricochet, or roquet-croquet, on all the balls in the game, it has only one more stroke, when its tour terminates.

88. If a ball, in executing the croquet, FLINCH from under the foot of the player, its tour terminates.[24]

89. A ball may decline to take its tour of play; or at any time leave it unfinished.[25]

90. The commencement of each new tour of play, restores a ball to all the privileges of the game.

[23] In either case, of rules 85 and 86, the slightest displacement will suffice.

[24] This termination of tour is absolute; and no point made by the playing ball after the *flinch* can be claimed. (See Rules under Roquet, Ricochet, and Running the Bridges.) The only exception to this, is when a rover *flinches* in executing the croquet, and strikes out against the starting stake,—an advantage that, under most circumstances, would be cheerfully declined.

[25] It would be irrational to deny it this privilege: since, if the play be insisted upon, a slight tap of the mallet will suffice to satisfy the conditions—leaving the ball where the player desires it to lie.

Making Double Points.

91. If a ball *run* two bridges by a direct blow of the mallet, it can take ground, *up to one mallet's length,* in any direction from the spot where it has rested.[26]

92. If a ball run a bridge, by a direct blow of the mallet, and at the same time toll the stake—or *vice versâ* —it can take ground in any direction, up to one mallet's length.

93. If a ball run *three* bridges, as above, it can take ground in any direction, *up to two lengths* of the mallet.

94. If a ball run two bridges, as above, and at the same time toll the stake — or *vice versâ* — it can take ground, *up to two lengths* of the mallet.[27]

Misplay.

95. If a ball be played out of its proper tour, and challenged before the play of another ball has commenced, the misplayed ball may be returned to its original place, or permitted to remain in that to which it has rolled; but the option belongs, *not to the player of the ball, but to the enemy.*

96. If a ball, played out of its proper tour, have gained any advantages for itself, or its friends, or done any injury to the enemy, the latter, duly challenging, may strip the misplayed ball of *any or all* of the advantages thus gained, and repair *any or all* of the damages sustained.[28]

[26] If the mallet's length should enable it to take ground on the reverse side of its next or *proper* bridge, it does not count as *running* the bridge; since that can only be done by a blow of the mallet, by roquet, croquet, ricochet, concussion, rebound, or roquet-croquet.

[27] The rule might be extended; but a ball is not likely to run more than three bridges at one time, or two with the tolling of the stake.

[28] This is to be done, by returning the misplayed ball to its original position; by moving any of the enemies that have been "bettered"

97. If a ball be played out of its proper tour, and *not* challenged in due time, the play will hold good.[29]

98. A ball played out of its proper tour, may be challenged at any time while in the act of play; the play stopped; and the forfeit required from it—as prescribed in the preceding rules.

99. If a ball be played out of its proper tour—whether challenged and mulcted of the damages, or not—it loses that tour; and must remain unplayed till the next after.[30]

100. A ball played, *by any other than its proper owner,* subjects the *player* to the same forfeits, as for playing out of turn.[31]

101. A ball played, by any other than its proper owner, subjects the player to the loss of one tour of play.[32]

102. A ball played, by any other than its proper owner, does not thereby forfeit its own tour of play.

103. If a ball, after having croque'd another, croquet it again during the same tour—before running a bridge or tolling the stake—it becomes liable to the same forfeits as a ball played out of turn.

104. If a rover take either croquet or roquet-croquet on the same ball, *twice during the same tour of play,* it

back into theirs; and allowing those of them, whose positions have been rendered worse, to remain. Also, by restoring *any or all* of the "spoilt" friends to the positions from which they have been displaced. The forfeit is a heavy one, but not unnecessarily so: since playing out of the proper time creates great confusion in the game, and should constitute a *crime* not to be lightly dealt with.

[29] The enemy, by not challenging, having forfeited his right to "take the damages."

[30] It does not actually *lose* a tour by playing out of its proper time. It has its play all the same, subject to the forfeit specified in the Rules.

[31] Of course, the enemy of the guilty, or mistaken, player, is his judge, and has the right to "lay the damages."

[32] The player only loses the play of his (or her) own ball—having already taken the tour on the wrong one.

becomes liable to the same forfeits as a ball played out of turn, and must terminate its tour whenever challenged.

105. A ball accidentally displaced, either by a back stroke of the mallet or otherwise, may be returned to where it was lying, or left on the spot into which it has rolled; but the option belongs, not to the player who has caused the accident, but to the enemy.[33]

106. If a ball, accidentally displaced, pass through its proper bridge, or strike the turning stake at the proper time for tolling it, the bridge is *run*, and the stake tolled —if the enemy so decide.

107. If a ball, in its progress over the ground, be interrupted by any of the players, it may either remain where it has rested after the interruption, or be carried to the most distant part of the arena,—in the direction in which it was rolling—at the option of the enemy.

Barriers and Boundaries.

108. A ball driven over the boundary may be brought back into the arena—in the shortest right line from the point where it has been *found lying*—and placed twelve inches inside the boundary line.[34]

---

[33] *Flukes* made by roquet, ricochet, or concussion, are not *accidental displacements.*

[34] There is a Rule directing the ball to be placed on the arena *at the point where it rolled off.* This is deficient. Why? Who knows *where* the ball rolled off? Who saw it? Perhaps no one: since nobody cares to note the course taken by a croqu'ed ball on its journey "up the country." The shortest right line—from the spot where the ball is found to the proximate boundary—is the perpendicular; and this will hold good, whether the boundary be a curved or straight line. The restored ball may be *placed* close to the line, with the privilege of taking twelve inches inside it. In like manner, if there be an obstacle in the arena—a tree, shrub, or even a flower-bed—forming an obstruction to the proper play of a ball, it may be carried twelve inches clear of the obstacle, on either side of it, *but not nearer to the*

109. A ball driven over the boundary should be returned to the arena, and *placed*, before the play proceed.

110. If a playing ball lie contiguous to a stake, or one of the piers of a bridge—so that it cannot be properly struck by the mallet—a blow given to the stake or rod, driving the ball by concussion, will count as if the ball itself had received the blow.

111. If a ball lying contiguous to a stake, or one of the piers of the bridges, be displaced by the concussion of another ball striking the stake or rod, the displacement remains good; but the playing ball (if it be one) makes no point in the game—unless the ball displaced may at the same time have been roque'd or ricoche'd.

The Rover.

112. The *Rover*—made so by a direct blow of the mallet—must continue its play from the *spot*.

113. The rover—made so otherwise than by a direct blow of the mallet—must continue its play from the place into which it has been rolled.

114. The rover—and it only—may execute the roquet-croquet.[33]

115. The rover can roquet-croquet the same ball, *only once during the same tour of play*.

116. The rover may strike the same ball, any number of times during the same tour; but only the first stroke makes a roquet, giving the right to continue the play.

bridge or ball intended to be played at. It must be *placed* before the play proceed.

This last regulation may be regarded as a *rule;* but as a correct croquet-ground does not contemplate obstacles of the kind referred to, it is not given among the absolute "edicts" of the game.

[35] Some of the Rules, under the heading of The Rover, have been given elsewhere. They are here partially repeated: as the privileges of the rover have been hitherto so ill-defined, that it is desirable they should be thoroughly understood. See Note 18.

117. The rover may croquet any ball in the game; but only once during the same tour.

118. If the rover has croque'd a ball, it cannot roquet-croquet it during the same tour.

119. If the rover has roquet-croque'd a ball, it cannot croquet it during the same tour.

120. If the rover make a ricochet, it may roquet-croquet all the ricoche'd balls; but it must proceed from one to the other in the order in which they have been ricoche'd, without any intervening play.

121. If the rover make a ricochet, it may croquet some of the balls and roquet-croquet the others; but it must proceed in the order in which they have been ricoche'd, without any intervening play.

122. The rover cannot *run* a bridge—having run them already in making the *grand round*. It may pass through a bridge, but this makes no point in the game.

123. The rover cannot toll the turning stake—having done so already. It may strike against the stake; but the contact makes no point in the game.

124. The rover may be *struck out* against the starting stake by a blow of the mallet, by roquet, ricochet, concussion, rebound from a fixed object, recoil from the person of its own player, or that of a friend, by flinch, by croquet, or the roquet-croquet of another rover. When this event occurs—either by chance or design—the rover terminates its existence, and is thenceforth a *dead ball*.

125. A *dead ball*, on being declared dead, is to be instantly taken up, and *carried* out of the arena.

126. When all the *friends* of a side have struck out, they can call " Victory."

COX AND WYMAN, PRINTERS, GREAT QUEEN STREET, LINCOLN'S-INN FIELDS.

CPSIA information can be obtained at www.ICGtesting.com
Printed in the USA
BVOW08s0048190614

356800BV00011B/212/P